MW01171810

The

EXECUTIVEPRENEUR

The Executivepreneur
Making Money Beyond Your Salary

Tayisha M. Beard
Eight One Eight Publishing

All rights reserved. No part of this publication may be reproduced, distributed, or transmitted in any form or by any means, including photocopying, recording, or other electronic or mechanical methods, without the prior written permission of the publisher, except in the case of brief quotations embodied in critical reviews and certain other noncommercial uses permitted by copyright law.

This book is a work of nonfiction. The author has made every effort to ensure the accuracy of the information herein. However, the author and publisher assume no responsibility for errors, omissions, or damages caused by the use of the information contained herein. The author is not a financial advisor, tax attorney, or investment consultant and is not giving financial or investing advice. All information is provided based on what has worked for the author and for clients. Results and outcomes are not guaranteed.

Paperback ISBN: 979-8-9888581-4-0
Digital ISBN: 979-8-9888581-3-3

DEDICATION

I dedicate this book to my family and friends who have supported me on this journey to find my purpose or, as I call it, "finding my true work." I could not have done this without my husband, children, parents, and siblings. Thank you for your words of wisdom and advice along the way.

READ THIS FIRST

Thank you for buying and reading my book. As a special bonus, scan the QR code to receive the first two chapters of the audiobook.

The

EXECUTIVEPRENEUR

MAKING MONEY BEYOND YOUR SALARY

TAYISHA M. BEARD

CONTENTS

PREFACE

Growing up, I had low self-esteem and very little confidence that my financial situation would change from humble beginnings. I thought that getting by and merely existing was enough in life. It was rare to see women succeed independently and take their financial well-being into their own hands. I knew if I wanted something different than what I had seen over the years, I would have to take on the responsibility of making it happen and paving the way.

How scary is it for a shy, teenage African American girl? Fear held many back where I was from, and I was willing to risk it all to be the groundbreaker. While climbing the corporate ladder all the way to the top, I started to think about my legacy and generational wealth for the children. I realized that I was living a great life but not preparing for the next several generations after me. I started to shift my focus from making money to manifesting wealth. I did this by investing in many ways, the biggest being in real estate. I watched my net worth begin to grow at a rapid pace and my circle of influence change as I shifted my mindset.

If you are serious about creating your legacy, I encourage you to take this journey with me as I show you how I converted my six-figure wages into wealth.

INTRODUCTION

Let's talk about it. You've done it! Whether you climbed the corporate ladder or took the less traditional route, you navigated the barriers. You broke through the proverbial glass ceiling, gender, age, and racial gaps to stake your claim among women who earn over six figures. You should have a ton of equity and ownership built up for yourself, right?

Then why do you have this nagging feeling of wanting more for yourself? You are building value for so many others but lack ownership and assets for yourself. You are living a good quality life, but you realize that you won't be around forever. What is the legacy you will leave behind for your children? As you start to evaluate your relationship with money, you come to grips with the fact that you have spent way too much, saved some, and invested very little.

Yes, you should be proud of all your accomplishments. However, if making six figures doesn't make you feel like you are living an upper-class lifestyle but rather like Cinderella cleaning the stone floors, and you still feel like you are not doing enough to secure your financial future, you are not alone. Your intuition is accurate.

It doesn't take a rocket scientist to know that the utility of a six-figure income depends on your location and personal demographics. Making $100k in Tennessee will most definitely feel more comfortable than living in DC or New York. Having children or uncommon healthcare costs will also impact how far your income goes. But that is not the whole story.

According to the Bureau of Labor Statistics, due to the cumulative rate of inflation, you would need to earn $129,000 today compared to $100,000 ten years ago to have the same purchasing power.

If the increased cost of living is not enough, you also have to consider what is happening to traditional investment and savings options. For example, we were taught that contributing to our 401(k) plan or an IRA was an intelligent option. However, your contributions have limits. The IRS increased the maximum limits, but if you plan to truly be financially free, the limits are a drop in the bucket if you consider the cost of living, fees, and taxes on those funds or investments over time. These factors do not include fluctuations in the stocks during your holding period.

Unless you live under a rock, none of this is new information. So, why don't you invest in other options? Why do you avoid diversification of assets and income? I'm glad you asked!

It's not just you! Did you know that in 2018, less than half of women investors invested outside their retirement plan? The percentage of women engaging in outside investing has increased, but it still lags behind that of their male counterparts. Additionally, this data reveals that women investors often outperform men in terms of investment returns. According to a study conducted by Wells Fargo, women were better at taking on less risk and reaching higher returns. You would think the positive data would make its way through the network and encourage more investing by women.

The issue is that women face real concerns about investing and must overcome barriers similar to those encountered in the workforce or when starting a business.

The first has been the income problem. There is a misperception about how much you actually need to start investing.

The second barrier is a knowledge problem. The investment industry caters to men, and investments are often encouraged in areas where women feel less confident in making decisions.

Finally, women are traditionally risk-averse and often believe investing requires more risk. Women are playing a game of catch-up when it comes to finances and money and do not want to risk losing what they have worked so hard to earn. To make matters worse, the statistics are even more alarming for Black women!

Sound familiar? If anything you read speaks to you, and you are ready to create generational wealth, build your asset portfolio with confidence, make passive income, and break through your fear of investing, you are in the right place! I will teach you how to change your mindset and finances to create a lasting impact over your time and retirement through financial freedom.

Being an Executivepreneur marks a shift in your mindset as you realize the value of your time and prioritize family and self-care. At this step, you begin to invest and circulate your wealth, whether through a purposeful side business or real estate ventures, with a focus on creating generational wealth and passive income.

In this book, you will learn how I built my real estate portfolio, community, and net worth by investing in myself. Begin your journey by gaining perspective on your current state of mind, career success, your relationship with money, and examining the importance of self-care. Learn how to maximize your corporate benefits and gain an understanding of good debt versus bad debt. Then work through the Asset MultipliHER Framework and Blueprint and Work-Life Balance Sheet. You do not have to choose between your executive role or building your business and legacy. You can do both, and I will show you how!

YOUR MONEY MINDSET

*"If you don't have passive income,
then income is passing you by."*

*I*f you're like me, you may have thought that making a great salary would solve so many problems. Maybe you began a sentence or two with "If only I were rich then . . ." Throughout our adolescent and young adult lives, we are told that we should work hard and get a "good job." To most, a good job meant a salary that hovered around six figures or more. Six figures meant you made it up the corporate ladder and to the upper class. You are rich. Then reality sets in.

You buy the house and the new car. Business attire is a must. Eating out becomes a habit because you are so focused on the next raise or promotion. The more you make, the more you spend. After all, being upper class comes with expectations. Before long, that six-figure income feels like you are living paycheck to paycheck. Am I wrong?

As you continue to read, I want you to keep in mind that being rich and being wealthy are two different things. While being rich can support you for a lifetime, it is wealth that will support your family for generations. One gets the bills paid, and the other gives you freedom beyond the money. Once you shift your mindset to wealth, things begin to look different. However, this shift in mindset takes a bit of reflection and starts with your relationship with money.

YOUR VIEW OF MONEY

How you view money is deep-seated in familial and cultural ties. For example, your belief in going to college and securing a good job with a big company most likely came from the values of your parents and grandparents. Decades ago, grandparents were loyal to one company and worked their entire careers at the same place. They were rewarded with a pension. Many of our parents followed that same path with some minor adjustments. For example, they had stock options and retirement plans instead of pensions. These generations believed in putting a percentage of money into savings. When they retired, they believed that savings would take care of them for the remainder of their years.

Depending on your age, you may have grandparents or great-grandparents who would reuse disposable items, stock up on odd food products, or never throw anything away. They did this because they lived through World War II, where they had food rations (yes, in the US). Couple that with trying to survive the Great Depression. You may have rolled your eyes when great-grandma gave you five dollars for Christmas, but that was a lot to her.

Culturally, you may experience the same thing. For example, when we accidentally break pottery, we throw it away. However, in ancient Japanese culture, the practice is to restore it. Another example is the dad or grandpa who insists on fixing every small appliance and lamp. This practice often stems from living in isolated rural areas where new appliances and parts were hard to come by.

So, where do your beliefs about money come from? Are you a woman who spends every dime you make because you have a fear that it will be taken from you if you don't? Do you pinch every penny in fear that you will need that money in the near future or never have enough?

We often have unrealistic views and an unhealthy relationship with money based on our past experiences and what we were taught. Now is the time to work through that. Shift your thinking.

Money is a tool. It is time to learn how to use it to get what you want. The next image is a chart with the average relationship between women and money.

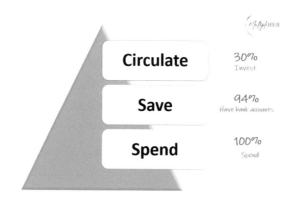

SCARCITY VERSUS ABUNDANCE

If you have a negative relationship with money, it most likely stems from a scarcity mindset. This is the belief that you have limited resources available to you. You think that there are only so many pieces to the pie, and once you have your share—that is it—not realizing more pies can be made. The wealthy know that their potential returns on investments are boundless.

The secret to wealth is the wealthy have seven or more streams of income, with their salary being the primary source. They spend money by purchasing assets with increasing value in cash flow over time, bringing in additional revenue. Understanding the value of time is important to realize that wealth is built over time, not overnight.

Here are the most common streams of income:

1. Primary Income
2. Second Income or Spouse Income
3. Investment Income
4. Rental Property
5. Side Business
6. Limited or General Partnerships
7. Acquisitions

The abundance mindset is where you believe in boundless opportunities. There is enough for everyone; life and money are not zero-sum games with winners and losers. When you have an abundance mindset, you are not saying, "I can't." Instead, you are asking, "How can I?"

Of course, changing your mindset can take some practice. And the abundance mindset does not advocate that you spend recklessly. When investing, operating from an abundance mindset is about looking for opportunities and grabbing them when they pop up.

If you want to work on your mindset and shift to abundance, start with gratitude and authenticity. Abundance is about being thankful for what you have so that you can attract new possibilities. Be authentic by embracing the beginner mindset and dropping the ego. Commit to growth and learning by taking classes, watching webinars, reading, or attending seminars. Finally, work to use positive affirmations framed in the present, like *I am creating generational wealth by purchasing real estate.*

Remember to avoid the "I can't" and focus on "how can I?" I purchased my first rental property in 2009 for $35k at twenty-eight. I had no training, no mentor—just me trying to figure out this wealth game. I started to pay off debt and wanted to own something outside of my first starter home. Before my shift in mindset, I spent more money shopping, traveling, getting back into debt, and "keeping up with the Joneses." I had nothing to show but a closet full of clothes, handbags, and great memories of spending lavishly.

Did I say it was fun, and I enjoyed every minute of it? Well, I did! However, I look back now and think of how much real estate or assets I could have purchased over that ten-year period and what that would mean to my net worth now. My eyes opened in 2019, and you will see later in the book what attributed to my mindset shift and how I went from one property from 2009-2020 to adding six additional properties from 2020-2023. This took me to over seven figures in real estate investments. I went from retail therapy to financial freedom when I chose to shift my energy and thoughts.

Once you understand where your view of money comes from and shift your mindset, you will realize that your six-figure income and working for someone else might make you rich will not offer freedom. You will shift your thought process to focus on balanced career success and long-term self-care. You can start this shift in mindset by saving three to six months of your salary in an emergency fund if you do not have one. From there, it's time to circulate your money into cash-flowing assets. Someone has to take the leap of faith to create a legacy for your last name. Will it be you? I've decided that it's me for the Beard legacy. It is not how you start; it's how you finish. But you do have to start somewhere.

What You Can Do RIGHT NOW:

1. Reflect on your relationship with money to determine if you are a spender, a saver, or a circulator.
2. If you are a spender, what are you spending your money on? Start a list to determine where your money is going.
3. Ask yourself, is it an asset or a liability?
4. If it's an asset, your net worth should increase after you make the purchase. Determine whether your net worth is growing or declining.
5. How many streams of income do you have? One stream of income is not enough; it is too close to being broke. If you put all your eggs in one basket, you could lose it all. You should seek equity, not just a salary.
6. What other streams of income can you create that will contribute to the left side of your personal financial statement?
7. Make better decisions when spending your money. Set a budget for yourself and a goal for creating wealth. Remember, anything beyond your emergency fund should be put to work for you, generating cash flow or building equity.

CAREER SUCCESS AND LONG-TERM SELF-CARE

"A career is wonderful, but you can't curl up with it at night."

~ MARILYN MONROE

*I*f you are reading this, the chances are you have discovered that your early visions of success lack the wonder and joy of the fairytale we were given as young girls. You were told you could have it all, but you were not given a blueprint on how to make it all happen. After all, you are smart and driven to succeed. You have a fire in your belly and made it to the top. It may have never dawned on you that the idea of being a successful career woman while having a family, social life, and personal time could be a soul-crushing experience. One dilemma was choosing between calling off an important kick-off meeting and finding someone trustworthy to care for your sick child, which happened more than expected.

Faced with layoffs or promotions, parental responsibilities, and house chores, it is no wonder short fuses and mental exhaustion have become the norm. What nobody ever mentioned is that work-life balance isn't balance. The pendulum swings from one side to the other. When we feel it in our grasp, we shift to give our family the affection and attention they need. Then we swing back.

The reality is we can have it all, just not at the same time. There is such a thing as a work-life balance, but mine will look different from yours. Balance does not mean equal! You have to create your own work-life balance and be okay with adjusting it as needed without permission. Give yourself grace and adjust as often as you feel the need to. If you don't and you avoid self-care, you will not be successful at work or in life.

I know. My idea of success and self-care changed for me in 2019 after waking up with chest pains in the middle of the night. I was awakened by my heart rate beating 170 beats per minute. My husband rushed me to the emergency room, where the doctors quickly connected me to an EKG machine and ran a CT scan to determine what was happening to me. After several tests, I was sent home and told to take an aspirin. The doctors told me there was nothing they could do to stop a heart attack from happening if that was what I was experiencing. I was so scared to go home and cried throughout the night.

After finally dozing off, I woke up and thanked God for being alive and feeling better. It all had to be a mistake, is what I said to myself. I got out of bed and headed out to work my normal day in the office. The day was good, and I made it back home to get dinner started. About 5:30 p.m., the chest pains started again, and I began to have trouble breathing. I was sweating profusely, and I started to lose consciousness. I picked up the phone to call my mother, and once again, I was being driven to the emergency room. This is the second consecutive day in the ER.

This time, I was admitted to the hospital so the doctors could have time to bring in a specialist. There were pulmonologists, cardiologists, and many other doctors running tests, all to determine that my physical health was fine. I was diagnosed with anxiety attacks, also known as panic attacks. I could not believe that stress and not taking care of myself were causing my body to feel and react this way.

I did a lot of self-reflection and asked myself some hard questions about the decisions I had made for myself and my family. The hardest question I asked myself was: *If something had happened to me during those nights in the hospital, how would the future of my family, children, and legacy have been impacted?* The answer was clear—I wasn't prepared. I had wasted precious time and money on things that were not as important as my family, and I didn't have enough assets or equity to leave a legacy for my children.

Yes, I have life insurance, stocks, savings, and 401(k), but what happens when that runs out after a few years? Would my family lose all the ground that was made when I was there to contribute? We are not here on this earth forever. If you want to build a legacy and create wealth, the time is now! Don't wait! It is time to build ownership for yourself.

BEING SELFISH

Culturally, and some would argue genetically, women are nurturers. It is in our blood to be empathic, helpful, and organized. Unconscious biases dictate that it is okay to have a successful career, but it should be secondary to taking care of the nuclear family. Sure, some responsibilities have shifted over the decades, but recent studies still tell us that women carry the burden of domestic work like cleaning, planning, grocery shopping, and parental duties.

Self-care is viewed as a luxury. Spending money or time on massages, a date night, a girl's night out, or even reading a good book is often hard to justify. And even if we manage to have the time and money, self-care can cause guilt or inevitably get interrupted by one person or another. Just me?

Here's the thing. To create generational wealth, true career success, and enjoy long-term positive self-care, you are going to have to be a little selfish. I am not talking about buying the luxury brand handbag or taking the yoga retreat. I am talking about assessing what you need versus what you want and then setting achievable goals to get there.

If I were to ask you what you need or want more of, what would your answer be? I would bet it would be time. Time is our most valuable resource; we seem to give it away faster than battery-operated toddler toys from Christmas.

You need and want more time. Got it? Now, if I were to make a second guess about what you need and want, I would say you *need* and *want* a way to have a more secure future that doesn't depend on working until retirement age to receive social security. You want and need financial freedom. However, I would guess you are afraid to take movement in any direction because you fear it will take more of your time or money.

Here's the thing: You don't have to invest more time or extraordinary amounts of money to build generational wealth. The three methods I use to make more money, which doesn't require lots of time or an endless bankroll, are real estate, stocks, and either limited partnerships or business equity deals. While you don't need extra time or significant liquidity to start, you will need to establish boundaries and the ability to be a bit selfish.

What You Can Do RIGHT Now:

1. *Evaluate What Self-Care Looks Like*: Self-care isn't retail therapy. I promise! Self-care is about time and resetting your energy. What makes you feel at peace and relaxed? Could it be a walk in nature or a soothing bath? Maybe yoga or curling up with a good book? Self-care doesn't require spending money.

2. *Block Out Time*: Utilize your Google or Outlook calendar to block off your work meetings as well as your self-care and personal time. I bet you never thought that you would have to schedule self-care time, but you do, and you should. Time and life move fast, and if you don't schedule time for yourself, everything and everyone will seem to take priority over you. As the airline attendants say, put your mask on first! You create value for others daily; it is now time to create ownership for yourself. That ownership can be ownership of your time, your finances, your legacy, or your career.

3. *Delegate*: A successful career is at its highest when you are mentally well. Learn to delegate and empower your team to be leaders in the company. Behind every good leader is a team that has the support and tools they need to be successful. You cannot do it alone, so stop trying. We all need help to be able to help others. While you are at it, delegate at home too!

4. *Set Boundaries*: Learn to say no. Successful women tend to take everything in stride and often feel saying no is equal to failure. However, setting boundaries is the ultimate power move in taking your time back. What can you say no to?

5. *Prioritize Your Tasks*: Highly successful are task masters. They do it by planning the night before. Multitasking isn't a thing. So, figure out which tasks are urgent, which tasks are complicated, and which ones can be completed in less time. Do the easy ones first, then the urgent ones, then the ones that require deep focus.

Focus on one task at a time and only move on once the current task is done. This means setting boundaries. If someone says, "It's an emergency," you need to consider what an emergency consists of. Does it require the police, fire department, or doctor? Most often, it can wait a bit.

Setting boundaries and evaluating and prioritizing your time will open your eyes to what is a priority in that moment. You will begin to see the difference between good and bad uses of your time. From there, you will learn the power of saying no and not today.

03

GOOD DEBT VERSUS BAD DEBT

"Debt is one person's liability but another person's asset."

*M*anaging your finances is crucial to achieving long-term financial success as an executive woman earning a six-figure income. One of the most critical elements of financial management is understanding your relationship with debt. There is "good debt" and "bad debt." We are most familiar with bad debt. We have an intimate relationship with it. But what is good debt?

Good debt refers to borrowing money to invest in assets that have the potential to appreciate in value or generate long-term income. It is a strategic financial tool that can enhance your financial position over time. Typically, good debt is associated with lower interest rates and offers opportunities for growth and wealth creation. Some examples of good debt are:

- **Education:** Investing in your education is often considered good debt. You enhance your knowledge, skills, and earning potential by obtaining advanced degrees or certifications. The returns on this investment can outweigh the initial borrowing costs. We will save the debate on student loans for another time, as they could be good or bad. However, no matter where or how the knowledge or information is obtained, it is crucial to execute on the information. If you invest in enhancing your knowledge personally or professionally and don't execute, it turns into bad debt.

- **Real Estate:** Purchasing a property intending to rent or sell for profit can be a sound investment. Real estate has historically appreciated in value over time, making it an attractive option for building wealth and cash flow.

- **Starting a business:** If you have an entrepreneurial spirit and are ready to branch out with a great service or product, borrowing money to start a business can be good debt. Make sure that whatever business you start aligns with your purpose in life. Remember, it's not how much money you make; it's how you make money. All money is not good money. Starting a business for the wrong reasons can quickly become bad debt.

A financial example of good debt looks something like this:

You take out a low-interest loan of $50,000 to start a business. Assuming an interest rate of 5% over five years, the total interest paid would be $6,918. However, if your business generates a net profit of $15,000 per year, the investment in the business could result in a positive return.

Conversely, our familiar foe, bad debt, involves borrowing money to fund purchases or expenses that do not contribute to your financial well-being or generate income. It is often characterized by high-interest rates and can lead to a cycle of debt, negatively impacting your financial health in the long run. We know what bad debt looks like; here are the most common examples:

- **Consumer Goods:** Borrowing or spending money to purchase depreciating assets, such as luxury cars, expensive gadgets, or extravagant vacations, falls under bad debt. These purchases do not generate income or appreciate in value, leading to a net loss over time.
- **Credit Cards:** Using credit cards without the means to pay off the balance in full each month can result in accumulating high-interest debt. Impulsive spending and relying on credit cards for everyday expenses can quickly lead to financial instability. Additionally, we can be caught off guard by their variable interest rates, leading to owing more than we borrowed with long-term costs.

An example of bad debt may hit close to home:

Suppose you have $10,000 in credit card debt with an interest rate of 20%. If you only make minimum payments, it will take you over thirteen years to pay off the debt, with total interest paid amounting to

$12,600. This example highlights how high-interest debt can accumulate and become a significant financial burden. What's worse is if you maxed out your credit card when the interest rate was 16%, and that rate is now 26%. In 2023, this has been the reality.

Sometimes the line between good and bad debt can be blurry. For example, as mentioned, student loans can fall on either side. Owning a house is another one. You will hear real estate brokers and others claim that owning real estate is ALWAYS a good investment. In reality, owning real estate can be good or bad, depending on the circumstances. Yes, real estate is one of the best investments to have if you go in with your eyes open. Let's talk about it.

OWNING A HOUSE: GOOD OR BAD DEBT?

Whether owning a house is considered good or bad debt depends on various factors, including your financial circumstances, the housing market, the purpose of the property, the location, and the condition. It can be a good debt because:

- **You Are Buying a Home as an Investment:** Purchasing a property in an area with a high potential for appreciation can be considered good debt. If the property generates rental income or is expected to appreciate significantly over time, it can contribute to long-term wealth creation.
- **You Are Building Equity:** Making mortgage payments builds equity in your home, which can be leveraged for future investments or financial emergencies. Building equity can be a smart financial move, especially if the interest rates on the mortgage are reasonable.

However, buying or owning a home can be bad debt if:

- **You Overspend on Housing:** Purchasing a home that stretches your budget and leads to financial strain can be categorized as bad debt. If the mortgage payments become unaffordable or hinder your ability to save and invest, it may negatively impact your financial well-being.
- **You Don't Do Your Homework:** Understanding the location and condition of the property you purchase is crucial. Some investors may waive inspections or fail to do research only to find that there are significant structural issues or that the property is located in an area that has undesirable future plans or uses.

Women are 50% of the population, but less than 30% of real estate investors are women. Why is that? One reason is that many women don't even see it as a possibility for themselves. Another big reason is FEAR. I don't want to scare you away from real estate because there is always an upside; it just depends on your long-term goals.

One of the biggest fears in real estate investing is women don't want to get into huge debt to buy a property. The reality is you do not have to use your money! For example, buying your primary residence is a great way to start investing in real estate. You put a minimal down payment and then enjoy the home for a few years. Eventually, you sell it and use the equity to move up or keep it as a rental and take out equity to buy another home.

Understanding the distinction between good and bad debt is vital to building long-term financial stability. Good debt, such as investments in education or real estate, can contribute to wealth creation, while bad debt, like consumer goods and credit card debt, can hinder financial progress. Depending on various factors, owning a house or real estate can be good or bad debt. Being aware of rising interest rates on credit cards and their potential impact is crucial to avoid falling into a cycle of high-interest debt. You can navigate debt wisely and secure a prosperous financial future by making informed financial decisions. So, forget those consumer goods and impulse purchases under the guise of self-care. Start focusing on good debt and finding ways to leverage what you have. You can start by maximizing your corporate benefits and salary.

Then, consider other things that you can do from a personal standpoint.

What You Can Do RIGHT Now:

1. *Restrict Credit Card Use*: Use your revolving accounts (credit cards) only as needed, or if you are disciplined with a points or rewards strategy. This involves using your credit cards for the reward benefits and then paying off the full amounts each month. It's a great strategy if you are truly disciplined and adhere to it. If not, you may end up creating more high-interest debt for yourself while chasing reward points.

2. *Pay Down Your Bad Debt*: If your revolving debt is over 30 percent of the credit limit, create a plan to pay down the accounts one account at a time.

3. *Complete a Personal Finance Statement*: I encourage you to complete a personal financial statement every month. Once you spend a few hours completing the first statement (if you have never done it before) or working off a statement you completed some time ago, updating it monthly should take only thirty minutes or less. This will enable you to see if your net worth is increasing, decreasing, or staying consistent. Good debt will make you money, while bad debt will take money away. Your personal finance statement will serve as a mirror for you to look into every month, revealing your financial truth.

4. *Do or Redo Your Budget*: So many have a budget, but it isn't accurate. Take time to track every penny you spend over the course

of a month. Compare your actual spending to your budget. Were you off? What can you adjust to free up money for investing?

5. *Tithing*: Ten percent of your earnings should be given back to support local charities, a church, or someone in need. Malachi 3:8-9 discusses how a person can rob God in their contributions to tithes. Malachi 3:10 states, *"Bring the whole tithe into the storehouse, that there may be food in my house. Test me in this,"* says the Creator, *"and see if I will not open the floodgates of heaven and pour out so much blessing that you will not have room enough for it."* Don't hold on to what does not belong to you when it comes to tithing.

"Give, and it will be given to you: good measure, pressed down, shaken together, and running over, will be given to you." - Luke 6:38.

04

MAXIMIZING YOUR CORPORATE BENEFITS

*"Money won't create success,
the freedom to make it will."*

~ NELSON MANDELA

*A*s a successful woman earning a six-figure income, optimizing your financial strategies to achieve long-term prosperity is crucial. I give you one word—Leverage.

In finance and investing, there is OPM or "Other People's Money." This term refers to borrowing capital from people or businesses to increase the returns of an investment. The act of using money that is not yours for investment is also called leverage. Using a mortgage to buy real estate is using OPM or leverage. However, corporate benefits like 401(k) matching also use OPM or leverage.

You might be familiar with some of these benefits. However, you might be unaware of others. I want to highlight taking full advantage of various corporate benefits beyond 401(k) plans. This can include stock purchase programs, Health Savings Accounts (HSAs), tuition reimbursements, company vehicle programs, travel benefits, life insurance policies, and more. By capitalizing on these resources, you can enhance your financial position and accelerate your journey toward financial freedom. So, let's dig in on the 401(k) first.

401(K) PLANS

One of the most valuable corporate benefits is the 401(k) plan. Take advantage of this tax-advantaged retirement account by contributing the maximum allowable amount, especially if your employer offers matching contributions. By doing so, you not only benefit from the power of compounding but also enjoy immediate returns through employer matching. Many companies will match up to 6% of the amount that you invest into your 401(k) account each month. Consider this OPM and utilize this benefit.

STOCK PURCHASE PROGRAMS

Many companies offer employee stock purchase programs (ESPPs), which allow you to buy company stock at a discounted price. By participating in these programs, you can leverage the potential appreciation of company shares while potentially benefiting from dividends. Of course, it's essential to evaluate the risks and rewards associated with your company's stock and diversify your investments accordingly. Some buy and sell these stock options regularly; others will buy and hold.

HEALTH SAVINGS ACCOUNTS (HSAS)

HSAs provide a triple tax advantage, making them an excellent tool for maximizing healthcare-related savings. Contributing to an HSA can help you reduce your taxable income, grow funds tax-free, and withdraw money tax-free for eligible medical expenses. Consider fully funding your HSA if it is available and strategically investing the funds for long-term growth.

TUITION REIMBURSEMENTS AND STUDENT LOAN PAYMENTS

If your employer offers tuition reimbursements or student loan payment assistance, take full advantage of these benefits. By leveraging your employer's support for education, you can enhance your skills, increase your earning potential, and potentially minimize the burden of student loan debt. I'm familiar with companies offering a maximum of $10,000 in reimbursements per year, provided you achieve a qualifying GPA or grade.

COMPANY VEHICLE PROGRAMS

Some companies provide vehicle programs that offer significant discounts, lease options, or maintenance coverage. Assess whether participating in such programs aligns with your transportation needs and financial goals. Leveraging company vehicle programs can free up capital for other investments and reduce your overall transportation expenses.

TRAVEL BENEFITS AND REWARD POINTS

Explore travel benefits your employer provides, such as reward points, discounted rates, or travel expense reimbursement. By optimizing these benefits, you can enjoy cost savings on personal and business trips, allowing you to allocate more funds towards investments or savings. Many savvy users rack up enough points to travel with their family of four on business class to Costa Rica for free!

LIFE INSURANCE POLICIES

Does your company offer life insurance policies as part of its benefits package? While the primary purpose of life insurance is to provide financial security for loved ones, certain policies, such as cash value or whole life insurance, can also serve as an investment tool. Evaluate the potential returns and tax advantages of such policies before deciding. If you have the option, this is a great tool the wealthy use to make other investments!

LEVERAGING YOUR PROFESSIONAL NET-WORK: UNLOCKING SOCIAL CAPITAL

In addition to the tangible corporate benefits discussed, executive women have another invaluable resource at their disposal: their corporate, workplace, or professional network. We often overlook the importance of social capital and the cultivation of a strong, like-minded network for both financial investment and personal growth.

If unfamiliar, social capital refers to the network of relationships, trust, and shared values that exist within a community or social group. It encompasses the connections, influence, and resources individuals can access through relationships. It is an intangible asset with significant value in both personal and professional spheres. When you build social capital, you enjoy:

- **Access to Opportunities:** A robust professional network can provide you with access to a myriad of opportunities. Whether it's potential business partnerships, investment deals, or career advancement prospects, your network can serve as a gateway to valuable connections and openings that might otherwise be difficult to access. By nurturing relationships within your industry or field, you increase the likelihood of being informed about and considered for new opportunities.

- **Knowledge Sharing and Mentorship:** A strong network allows for knowledge sharing and mentorship, creating an environment of continuous learning and growth. By connecting with individuals who possess expertise or experiences in areas that align with your interests, you can tap into their insights, gain valuable advice, and avoid potential pitfalls. Mentorship relationships can accelerate your professional development, provide guidance during challenging times, and broaden your perspective.

- **Collaboration and Support:** Collaboration is often a catalyst for innovation and growth. By fostering relationships with like-minded professionals, you can find opportunities for collaboration, joint ventures, and shared projects. Your network can provide support, encouragement, guidance, and practical assistance when needed. Having a solid network of individuals who understand your challenges and aspirations can help you navigate obstacles and celebrate shared successes.

- **Influence and Reputation Building:** Your network can enhance your influence and help shape your professional reputation. Engaging with respected individuals in your industry can lend credibility to your ideas and initiatives. Building relationships with influencers or thought leaders can amplify your voice and increase your visibility within your field. By associating yourself with reputable professionals, you can enhance your personal brand and open doors to new opportunities.

Beyond the social and professional benefits, your network can also play a pivotal role in financial investment through:

- **Deal Flow and Investment Opportunities:** By connecting with individuals well-versed in investment opportunities, such as angel investors, venture capitalists, or real estate professionals, you gain access to a broader range of potential investments. Your network can provide insights into emerging trends, lucrative ventures, and trusted investment opportunities that may not be widely available.
- **Syndicate Investments and Co-Investment:** Leveraging your network allows you to pool resources and engage in syndicate investments or co-investment opportunities. By joining forces with like-minded investors, you can diversify risk, increase your purchasing power, and access larger-scale investment opportunities beyond your individual capacity.
- **Due Diligence and Expertise:** Your network can provide a valuable source of due diligence and expertise. By tapping into the knowledge and experiences of professionals within your network, you can make informed investment decisions and minimize potential risks. Discussions, debates, and sharing insights within

your network can help you assess investment opportunities critically.

To leverage your professional network effectively, consider the following strategies:

- **Actively Engage and Contribute:** Engage in company and industry events, conferences, and networking opportunities to meet new professionals and expand your network. Actively contribute to conversations, share your expertise, and offer assistance to others. Building relationships requires genuine interest, active listening, and reciprocating support.
- **Seek Like-Minded Communities:** Join professional organizations, industry-specific or company groups, or online communities that align with your interests and goals. These communities provide a platform to connect with individuals who share similar aspirations, challenges, and values. Engaging with like-minded professionals can foster deeper connections and collaboration opportunities.
- **Cultivate Authentic Relationships:** Focus on building genuine relationships based on trust, respect, and shared values. Nurture these connections by staying in touch, offering support, and providing value whenever possible. Remember that networking is a two-way street, and genuine relationships are built on mutual trust and reciprocity.

Leveraging your corporate workplace or professional network is a powerful strategy for unlocking social capital and enhancing your financial investment potential. You gain access to opportunities, knowledge, collaboration, and support by cultivating a strong, like-minded network. Additionally, your network can serve as a valuable source of due diligence, expertise, and co-investment possibilities. Embrace the power of social capital, actively engage with your network, and build authentic relationships to reap the rewards both in terms of financial investment and personal growth.

Leveraging corporate benefits and OPM can be highly advantageous. However, adopting a strategic approach is crucial to maximize returns and minimize risks. Keep in mind that your path to generational wealth and financial freedom is like a fingerprint; it is unique to you and your goals. Keep the following in mind:

- **Diversify Investments:** Avoid concentrating your investments solely in your employer's stock or benefits. Diversification is vital to mitigating risk and achieving long-term growth. Allocate your investment portfolio across various asset classes, industries, and geographic locations to reduce exposure to any single investment.
- **Understand Tax Implications:** Before leveraging corporate benefits, thoroughly understand the tax implications associated with each benefit. Consult with a tax professional or financial advisor to ensure you optimize tax advantages and minimize potential tax liabilities.
- **Evaluate Investment Risks:** Assess the risks associated with each investment opportunity and weigh them against potential rewards. Conduct thorough research, seek expert advice when needed, and make informed decisions that align with your risk tolerance and financial goals.

Not every investment or benefit will suit everyone's needs. However, maximizing corporate benefits that make sense and leveraging OPM are essential strategies for building wealth and achieving financial independence. And you can never go wrong with investing in social capital!

Once you maximize your corporate benefits and start building social capital, you are ready to become an asset MultipliHER!

Are you ready to take full advantage of your benefits?

What You Can Do RIGHT Now:

1. *What Are You Missing?* Contact your HR department for a list of your benefits. This will allow you to see which benefits you are already taking advantage of and which ones you should be utilizing to their fullest extent. If you can go back to claim or file for any benefits that you may have missed, do so with full confidence that you deserve them.

2. *Invest in Yourself:* If you are seeking personal and professional development, look for courses or higher education that can equip you with the tools to better perform your job and become your best self. Your company will appreciate you taking control of your career and self-development, which is why they may offer a tuition reimbursement program to their employees. Once you begin to tally all the benefits your company provides, you will perceive your overall salary as much higher than what you originally thought it to be.

Once you have maximized your corporate benefits, it is time to expand!

05

THE ASSET MULTIPLIHER FRAMEWORK AND BLUEPRINT

*"Everything is within your power,
and your power is within you."*

~ JANICE TRACHTMAN

*B*y now, you do not need to be told that you are intelligent and have resiliency, power, and determination. Those things are what helped you secure your six-figure job. But you broke glass ceilings and reached the last rung in the corporate ladder to find what? When there is not another rung in the ladder, where do you go?

So many executive women mistakenly believe that is the end of the line. They believe to earn more or grow, you have to job-hop to another company. But there is another way!

When you become a MultipliHER, you will follow the framework and blueprint to take you from a corporate executive to an Enterpriser. The path takes you from Executive to Executivepreneur, Entrepreneur, and Enterpriser. Each step in the framework builds on the previous one. Take a look:

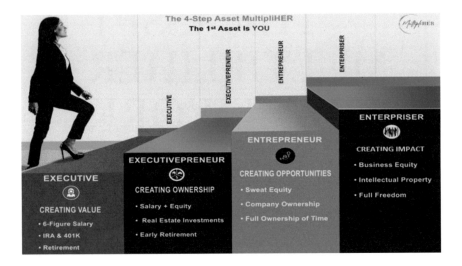

STEP 1 | EXECUTIVE

You are an executive-level woman earning a six-figure income and deserve an encore. You make an excellent salary but believe that you can save your way to wealth and plan to work until retirement age. You may be getting burned out and unsure of what's next for you. There is a better way to circulate your money and start to create wealth, but you don't have the blueprint or network to know what's available to you. If you have manifested this level of excellence, you are closer than you think to creating wealth and building your legacy. Dream Bigger!

You have dutifully set money aside in your IRA or 401(k) and taken full advantage of other corporate benefits like travel reward points and HSA accounts. The next step is to start creating ownership and wealth in addition to your corporate salary.

STEP 2 | EXECUTIVEPRENEUR

Step two marks a shift in your mindset as you realize the value of your time and prioritize your family and self-care. You begin to invest and circulate your wealth, whether through a side business or real estate ventures, with a focus on creating generational wealth and passive income. Your focus and ideas of what you want in life are starting to change. You realize your value and seek your "true work" or your purpose in life. Instead of trying to save your way to wealth, you have started to invest and circulate your money. Now, you are building your salary and your assets. You use your salary to accumulate passive investments and opportunities that do not take more time outside of your busy schedule.

You need a community of women and resources to take you further.

STEP 3 | ENTREPRENEUR

Here is where your business success and freedom define your personal success. You take ownership of your time and start creating opportunities for others. You take the leap and reclaim your independence as a full-time entrepreneur. You have the freedom to work from anywhere and control your income potential. By scaling your business and expanding your investments, you multiply your assets and generate a passive income that benefits not only you but also creates employment opportunities for others.

Do not mistake this step for a side hustle. This is where you build a business that will operate in your absence. Your business and assets can be handed down to the next generation. The goal is to build something fully operational that gives you freedom of time!

STEP 4 | ENTERPRISER

Here is where you are defined by your ability to build future leaders and contribute to your community. This step is about creating an impact. You embody the Proverbs 31 woman! Unfamiliar with scripture? You are a MultipliHER. You are the embodiment of "an industrious wife, a shrewd businesswoman, an enterprising trader, a generous benefactor, and a wise teacher."

Celebrate your success as an enterpriser, where you have achieved true financial independence and surpassed your high salary as an employee. Your business ventures and investments have provided wealth and allowed you to create a meaningful impact in your community. The office is yours, and you continue to build your network, leveraging it for further success. With the unwavering support of your like-minded network, you navigate the challenges of scaling your business and leave a lasting legacy of empowerment and abundance. Generational wealth starts with you, and your legacy will live on forever!

Are you ready to start your path to having full freedom of your time? Let's go!

What You Can Do RIGHT Now:

1. *Evaluate the Starting Line*: Know where you are. Not everyone starts at the same place. Are you a new executive, or have you been at it for ten years?

2. *See Your Vision*: Have a plan to get to your destination. It is more challenging to go from Executive to Enterpriser or A to D than it is to go from Executive to Executivepreneur or A to B. Set goals specific to you and what you want to achieve.

3. *Don't Compete With Anyone but Yourself*: Never be in a hurry where you skip steps or alter the process. Your path to wealth is unique to you, your experience, your resources, and your circumstances.

4. *Recognize This is a Journey*: Trust the process and take time to appreciate the journey of climbing the corporate ladder to your full freedom.

5. Take the Work-Life Balance Quiz (next chapter).

06

WORK-LIFE BALANCE SHEET

"We need to do a better job of putting ourselves higher on our own to-do list."

~ MICHELLE OBAMA

*E*very new endeavor requires a little reflection. This eight-question Work-Life Balance Quiz will take you down the path to determining your cash flow, assets, and time. You will be able to determine if you are creating passive income or if income is passing you by. This is the equity version of a balance sheet. The "work" speaks for itself; the "life" is the equity you create for yourself. At the end of the quiz, you will know where you are in your journey and how to go from earning a check to creating wealth.

THE QUIZ

Keep in mind that there are no right or wrong answers. We all have a different starting line. This quiz is for you to assess where you are and give you pause so you can reflect on where you want to go. You can also visit www.theworklifebalancesheet.com for the digital version of the quiz that will calculate your scores and to view your results immediately after completion.

Please check the appropriate box for each question. Remember to only select one answer per question.

1. **Are you a woman who has an income over six figures and who dreams BIG? (_____ points)**

   • Yes, I own and have shares in multiple businesses. **(4 pts)**
   • Yes, I own my own business and have multiple assets. **(3 pts)**
   • Yes, through my corporate job and some assets I own. **(2 pts)**
   • Yes, through my corporate job. **(1 pt)**

2. **Do you own real estate and other assets that generate passive income? (_____ points)**

   - Yes, I own multiple real estate investments and have limited partnerships in other businesses. **(4 pts)**
   - Yes, I own some investment properties that produce passive income. **(3 pts)**
   - Yes, I own my primary home and have 401(k)/IRA accounts. **(2 pts)**
   - I am buying my primary home, but I have no passive income assets. **(1 pt)**

3. **Do you have time for self-care and family? (_____ points)**

   - I have complete freedom to take care of myself and my family. **(4 pts)**
   - Full ownership of my time. **(3 pts)**
   - Some ownership of my time. **(2 pts)**
   - No ownership of my time. **(1 pt)**

4. **Taxed over 32 percent on your W-2 income? (_____ points)**

   - W-2 income does not apply to me, and I qualify for significant tax advantages from my asset portfolio. **(4 pts)**
   - I'm self-employed, have no W-2 income, and qualify for business related write-offs. **(3 pts)**
   - Taxed over 32 percent but have assets that depreciate and can apply for tax savings. **(2 pts)**
   - I'm taxed over 32 percent on my W-2 income. **(1 pt)**

5. **Can you maintain your lifestyle if you lose your executive job? (_____ points)**

- Yes, I have a passive and residual income from investments that can support me. **(4 pts)**
- Yes, my business can support me and my family through an active income. **(3 pts)**
- I have an emergency fund and assets that will support me for at least six to twelve months. **(2 pts)**
- I do not have an emergency fund and will need to find work within 30 days. **(1 pt)**

6. **Do you (or can you) easily create multiple streams of income? (_____ points)**

- Yes, I have multiple income streams today and plan to create more. **(4 pts)**
- Yes, I have created a path for multiple streams of income. **(3 pts)**
- Yes, I have created at least two streams of income. **(2 pts)**
- Only one stream of income, and I am unsure how to create more. **(1 pt)**

7. **Is your Net Worth consistent or improving every month? (_____ points)**

- My net worth increases every month through the equity in my asset portfolio. **(4 pts)**
- My net worth is improving at a great rate through the business that I operate daily. **(3 pts)**
- My net worth is climbing slightly every month. **(2 pts)**
- My net worth has remained consistent. **(1 pt)**

8. **Do you have a network of like-minded generational wealth builders that hold you accountable? (_____ points)**

- Yes, my circle is focused on physical and intellectual property. **(4 pts)**
- Yes, I have a circle of self-starters and entrepreneurs. **(3 pts)**
- I have a good circle of influence, but we speak more about career titles than generational wealth. **(2 pts)**
- I need a circle of influence. **(1 pt)**

Now that you have answered all 8 questions, take time to tally your score and get your results below. In order of each answer choice, please follow the chart below.

Level	Points
Enterpriser	4
Entrepreneur	3
Executivepreneur	2
Executive	1

EXECUTIVE (up to 15pts)

You are an executive-level woman earning a 6-figure income and you deserve an encore. You are a high-level earner and working to pay off debt, travel, and live the good life. You make a great salary but believe that you can save your way to wealth and plan to work until retirement age. You may be feeling burned out working long hours and not sure of your next career move. You may feel guilty about working as much as you do and not spending time with your family, children, or even your spouse. There is a better way to circulate your money, prioritize self-care, and start creating ownership for yourself. Don't worry, I've been there, and so have many other women. If you have manifested this level of excellence, you are closer than you think to creating wealth and building your legacy. Dream Bigger!

EXECUTIVEPRENEUR (16-23pts)

Your focus and ideas of what you wanted in life are starting to change. You realize your value and are seeking your "true work" or your purpose in life. You have identified that your time for your family and self-care is worth so much more than chasing money. Instead of trying to save your way to wealth, you have started to invest and circulate your money. You have either started a side business that fulfills you while balancing your career, or you may have invested in a rental property, beginning your journey to generational wealth and legacy. By taking advantage of tax avoidance strategies, you are now able to keep more of your income to invest in cash-flowing assets. You could never put a value on your time and have slowly begun to reclaim it, becoming more present when away from the office. Because of your mindset shift, you are a better leader for your company and your team. You believe in the ability to work smarter while balancing the effort of working harder. Now, you need a community of women and resources to propel you even further.

ENTREPRENEUR (24-31pts)

You have reclaimed your independence! Your time and your income potential are all in your hands. You have the ability to work from anywhere, and you should take advantage of this perk. Being an entrepreneur does not mean that it's easygoing, but what you put in is what you get out of it. So, there is still scaling to do. You have multiplied your assets and investment with passive income while you sleep. Your business or investments have made it possible to create employment opportunities for others in your community. You are thought of as a leader in the community that you serve and reside in. Your equity in assets and partnerships has well surpassed your high salary as an employee. Building your network will be the success of your net worth. You've got this!

ENTERPRISER (32+pts)

You embody the Proverbs 31 woman! You are a MultipliHER. You have created multiple streams of income and are coaching women leaders to do the same. You are a mentor to your peers and to the generations that come after you. You are known because of your wisdom and your charity work. Your external beauty is lagniappe. You live your life on purpose, and it is aligned with what the creator has designed for you. Your gift has made room for you. You are now being paid for your purpose. You never chase after money, but plant good seeds in good people and reap the harvest. Generational wealth starts with you, and your legacy will live on forever!

07

THE SECRET TO BUILDING WEALTH

*T*here is no secret to creating wealth. What you need to know is the wealthy do not exchange their time for money. They passively earn income while their assets do the heavy lifting. Much of their wealth is created through owning and investing in real estate.

The billionaire Andrew Carnegie once said that 90 percent of millionaires got their wealth through real estate investing. *Shark Tank* host Barbara Corcoran agrees, saying, "Buying real estate made me rich." Even the millionaire founder of Day Trading Academy, Marcello Arrambide, says, "Many businesses come and go, but there's one thing we'll always need—land."

Real estate is one of the few areas where you can invest a small amount of money and enjoy returns far beyond your initial capital input. It is much easier to use OPM for real estate investing than for any other asset class. The reason for this is that lenders know they have collateral that, over time, appreciates in value. You can borrow 80 percent or more of the property's price. The asset is tangible, unlike stocks and some other investments.

Yes, you should contribute to your retirement accounts and savings. However, I want to coach you on how to buy property using leverage and then how to leverage that property to buy another. Some use the "BRRRR" method (Buy, Rehab, Rent, Refinance, Repeat). Others invest in commercial properties, apartment buildings, or other properties. The key is to gain knowledge and confidence in making strategic choices and execute on what you have learned. The time is now!

What You Can Do RIGHT Now:

I want to bring awareness to a community of women leaders who are looking to network with each other, multiply their net worth, and build generational wealth for their families without having to choose between their careers and building their mental and physical real estate.

Remember: You are powerful and can be the change many people need to see. You can be a role model for those coming behind you. It is your time to multiply everything that you put your hands on. Dream bigger, multiply your asset portfolio, and create impact wherever you go.

Now that you have finished this book, hopefully, you are taking steps to align yourself with God's wisdom for your finances. A wealthy mindset is not given; it is taught. You can leave your legacy, your wealth, and all your worldly treasures to your children, but if they don't know what to do with it, the wealth stops there. If you were not born into wealth, be the one who starts building wealth for your family.

ACKNOWLEDGMENTS

I would like to take the time to thank all those who helped, supported, encouraged, and inspired me during the writing of this book. I would like to thank my husband, Henry, and children, Henry III and Kirstin, for their support and patience while I challenged myself during the writing process. This project wouldn't have made it past my internal thinking without my mentor, Jullien, and all those who believed in my vision and empowered me to fulfill my purpose of sharing my knowledge and experiences with other women. To my fellow P4P Alumni, thank you for holding me accountable. All of you were my motivation to keep going and getting the message about changing the wealth trajectory in our local communities and bridging the wealth gap for women of all races, especially brown and black women.

I pray this book reaches those who need the information at the right time and that they execute on it just as I did. To the generations of the Beard family that will one day read this book, I did this for you. Do not let the vision stop with me. Take what I have done and do greater. More than anything, ensure you are fostering your intellectual property, as you are the most valuable asset. Always invest in your mental real estate, and wherever you go, you will always have the full freedom to create your own legacy.

All glory goes to God, for it is He who has blessed me with everything that I have and everything that I am. In Him, I live, I move, and I have my being.

Thank you, and I love you!

ABOUT THE AUTHOR

My mission is to empower executive women to multiply their equity, not just their salary. I created the 4-Step Asset MultipliHER Framework, where I help executive-level women struggling with saving money rather than circulating money to successfully invest in cash-flowing assets. This is my passion, and I believe that God has blessed me to be a blessing to other women who have limited belief in themselves and in their power to build wealth.

I have been featured in the *Automotive News* magazine and was awarded the Leading the Way Award by a Fortune 500 company where I serve in senior-level leadership. I also serve as Market Leader for a real estate community in Louisiana and was a featured guest on the Multifamily Movement Mastermind in 2023.

I am originally from New Orleans, Louisiana, and currently reside in Gonzales, Louisiana, with my husband and two children. I earned my bachelor's degree from Louisiana Tech University, currently pursuing my MBA at Southern University, and am a member of the International Business Honors Society (Beta Gamma Sigma). I aim to be a role model of ambition and drive so that my children, as well as other women and minorities in the community, will know that they do not have to choose between success in business and a loving environment at home.

Made in the USA
Columbia, SC
29 September 2024

43303003R00040